party food

igloo

Published by Igloo Books Ltd
Cottage Farm
Sywell
NN6 0BJ
www.igloo-books.com

10 9 8 7 6 5 4 3 2 1

ISBN: 978 1 84817 634 8

Project Managed by R&R Publications Marketing Pty Ltd

Food Photography: R&R Photostudio (www.rrphotostudio.com.au)
Recipe Development: R&R Test Kitchen

Front cover photograph © Jupiter Images

Printed and manufactured in China

contents

introduction

Pick up most books with drink and cocktail recipes and you are often left wondering just what some ingredients are, and when it comes to making sugar syrups and turning a simple mixed drink into a major performance, most of us lose interest.

The tips and information that follow answer some of the questions many people ask about flavours, substitutes and simple alternatives to traditional ingredients.

HOW MUCH ICE

- Use small amounts of ice for cream-based drinks and sour-style drinks. Too much dilutes the drink and makes it taste mean and watery. More ice can be used in fruit-based drinks.

Crushed Ice

- Crushing ice can be a messy business. Use a food processor for this job. It's best to drop ice down the feed tube with the motor running so the ice doesn't get caught between the blade and the processor. Do not use a blender for crushing ice. Alternatively, ice can be placed in a heavy-duty plastic bag and crushed with a rolling pin or meat mallet. Do this on a shatterproof surface.

SUBSTITUTES

- Grenadine – this is a red-coloured pomegranate-flavoured syrup. It's very sweet. Raspberry cordial makes a good substitute.

- Sweet and sour mix is called for in some cocktail books. Use lemon or lime squash as a readymade alternative.

- Blue Curacao – make your own using equal parts of vodka and sugar syrup made using two parts sugar to one part water. Add blue food colouring and some orange oil or essence.

- Soda water – use sparkling mineral water instead.

- Cassis – when blackcurrant flavours are required for something like a Kir Royale, blackcurrant syrup can be used instead.

- Fruit liqueurs – if you haven't a particular flavour on hand, miniatures can always be bought instead of a big bottle. Alternatively, milkshake syrups can often be substituted where the flavour rather than the alcohol is important.

BASIC MIXES

- Sour – these are short drinks flavoured with lemon or lime juice. They can be made from almost any spirit.

- Collins – these are spirit-based and topped with a carbonated drink such as ginger ale or soda.

- Rickey – this is also a spirit-based drink mixed with lemon or lime juice and topped with soda water.

FLAVOURS

The flavours of various liqueurs and other mixes are often the cause of much debate and sometimes disagreement. This should set the record straight.

AMARETTO almond

ANGOSTURA BITTERS a high-octane rum-based flavour mix made from vegetable spices and colours with 44.7% alcohol

BENEDICTINE – brandy-based liqueur flavoured with herbs, spices and honey

BOURBON – the mash it's made from must contain at least 51% corn

COINTREAU brandy name for a Triple Sec orange-flavoured liqueur

CREME DE CACAO chocolate-flavoured liqueur

CREME DE CASSIS blackcurrant-flavoured liqueur

CREME DE FRAMBOISE raspberry-flavoured liqueur

CURACAO brand name for a Triple Sec orange-flavoured liqueur

DRAMBUIE whisky-based liqueur flavoured with honey and heather

GALLIANO liqueur flavoured with honey and vanilla

GRAND MARNIER cognac-based orange-flavoured liqueur

KAHLUA coffee-flavoured liqueur

KIRSCH cherry-flavoured liqueur

MALIBU rum-based coconut-flavoured liqueur

MIDORI melon-flavoured liqueur from Japan

PASTIS aniseed-flavoured liqueur

SAMBUCA liquorice-flavoured liqueur

SOUTHERN COMFORT whisky-based peach-flavoured liqueur

TEQUILA spirit distilled from maguey cacti

TIA MARIA rum-based coffee-flavoured liqueur

TRIPLE SEC colourless orange-flavoured liqueur

EQUIPMENT AND MEASURES

Making great cocktails or mixing delicious drinks doesn't mean you need a degree in drinks, with special skills and fancy equipment. Here are a few ideas that will make your drink mixing impressive and easily achieved.

GARNISHES

- Many zesters have a gadget on them for making strips of citrus peel without the pith. Simply run the shaped piece on the zester around the citrus to give a long piece of peel. This can be curled in a drink, tied, or used with other garnishes such as mint or cherries.

- Fruit pieces can be threaded onto toothpicks, small satay sticks or bamboo skewers. They can be put in the drink or balanced on the side of the glass.

- To sugar or salt the rim of a glass, dip the glass rim in lemon juice then into sugar or salt. Leave to dry before using to serve the drink in the glass.

- An attractive glass will usually make even the most ordinary drink look good. Long drinks can be served in large glasses while high-octane mixes are usually served in shorter glasses. Liqueurs or shots should be served in small chilled shot glasses. Champagne or methode champenoise glasses should be chilled before serving.

UTENSILS

- There is a fantastic range of cocktail shakers and utensils available to make mixing drinks easy. If you don't have the flash kits, don't let that stop you.

- Drinks can be shaken in a screw-top jar and strained through a fine sieve if necessary.

- Blenders are always good for drinks requiring crushed ice, fruit purees or when mixing in larger quantities.

MEASURES

- Cocktail kits often have measures in them or these can be bought separately.

- If you don't have any measures, remember a standard metric tablespoon is 15ml and a teaspoon 5ml.

- Conversions for cocktail measures:

1 oz	=	30ml	=	2 tablespoons
1 shot	=	45ml	=	3 tablespoons
1 cup	=	8oz	=	250ml

SPLASHES AND DASHES

There are about 36 dashes to 30ml. A dash or a splash in a drink recipe is like adding salt and pepper to food. You are seasoning to taste. If a recipe calls for a splash, that is slightly more than a dash but less than 7ml.

long, cool and quenching

Long, cool and quenching – it says it all. Drinks that are icy cold and perfect for sipping to refresh the body on a hot summer's day are what this chapter is all about. Savour the flavours of these drinks and drink with respect as fruity flavours can often mask the alcohol in a long, cool quencher.

Maui Lava Flow

(see photograph on page 10–11)

ice

30ml vodka

50ml coconut liqueur

60ml lime cordial

pineapple juice

6 strawberries

strawberry to garnish

1 Place ice in a screw-top jar or cocktail shaker. Pour in vodka, coconut liqueur, lime cordial and pineapple juice. Shake to combine and pour into a long glass. Hull strawberries and puree. Pour on top of pineapple mixture. Garnish with a strawberry.

Makes 1

Note: If you can't be bothered with the shaking for this drink, pour all the ingredients over ice in a long glass and mix with a long spoon to combine.

Spumante Cooler

(see photograph on page 10–11)

3 mint leaves

1 sugar cube

1 lime wedge

asti spumanti

1 Place mint leaves, sugar cube and lime wedge in a champagne flute. Top with asti riccadonna.

Makes 1

Harvey Wallbanger

(see photograph on page 10–11)

30ml vodka

15ml galliano

1 Pour vodka, galliano and orange juice over ice. Stir. Garnish with an orange slice and a cherry.

Makes 1

Tequila Sunrise

(right)

30ml tequila

125ml orange juice

1 teaspoon grenadine

slice of orange

cherry

1 Place ice in a tall glass. Add tequila and orange juice. Stir. Add grenadine into the middle of the cocktail. Allow the grenadine to sink slowly through the mixture. Garnish with a slice of orange and a cherry.

Makes 1

Pimm's

(see photograph on page 10–11)

45ml pimm's

lemonade

ginger ale

1 Pour pimm's and equal quantities of lemonade and ginger ale over ice. Stir. Garnish with an orange or lemon slice and a sprig of fresh mint and a cherry.

Makes 1

Tequila Lime and Soda

(right)

ice

30ml tequila

squeeze of fresh lime

soda

1 Fill a long glass with ice. Pour tequila over ice. Squeeze in lime juice and top with soda.

Makes 1

Note: For a change, top with cranberry juice if wished.

Pimm's Lim

(left)

ice

30ml pimm's

30ml lemon squash

tonic water

lemon slice to garnish

mint leaves to garnish

1 Place ice in a tall glass. Pour pimm's and lemon squash over and top with tonic water. Stir to blend flavours. Garnish with a lemon slice and fresh mint leaves.

Makes 1

Spirulina Pick-Me-Up

(right)

30ml gin

30ml vodka

125ml bottle spirulina

10ml kiwifruit juice

ice

kiwifruit slice to garnish

cherry to garnish

1 Pour gin and vodka into a long glass. Pour in spirulina and kiwifruit juice. Mix with a fork to combine and top with ice. Garnish with a slice of kiwifruit and a cherry.

Makes 1

Johnny's Navel

(left)

ice

30ml campari

30ml pimm's

tonic water

1 lemon slice to garnish

1 Place ice in a long glass. Pour campari and pimm's over ice and top with tonic water. Garnish with a lemon slice.

Makes 1

Note: If you prefer a sweeter drink, top this with lemonade.

Negroni
(back left)

30ml gin
15ml campari
15ml sweet vermouth
soda water
cherries

1 Pour gin, campari and sweet vermouth over ice. Top with soda water. Garnish with cherries.

Makes 1

Moscow Mule
(front left)

ice
lemon slices
30ml vodka
ginger ale
fresh lime juice
lime slice to garnish
sprig fresh mint to garnish

1 Fill a glass with ice, lemon slices, ice and more lemon slices. Pour vodka into glass. Add ginger ale to about 1cm from the top. Add a splash of lime juice. Garnish with a slice of lime and a sprig of mint.

Makes 1

Dark and Stormy
(back middle)

ice
30ml rum
ginger beer
orange slice to garnish

1 Fill a tall glass half full with ice, add the rum then fill the glass with ginger beer, stir gently and serve. Garnish with an orange slice.

Makes 1

Long Island Iced Tea
(middle right)

15ml vodka
15ml white rum
15ml gin
15ml tequila
15ml lemon cordial
30ml cola

1 Place ice in a tall glass. Add vodka, white rum, gin, tequila, cointreau and lemon cordial. Stir. Top up with cola. Stir again. Add a straw. Garnish with a lemon slice and a sprig of fresh mint.

Makes 1

Claridges
(back middle)

60ml orange juice
60ml champagne
30ml campari
orange slice to garnish

1 Pour orange juice and champagne into a chilled champagne flute. Top with campari and allow it to flow through to the bottom. Garnish with an orange slice.

Makes 1

Blue Lagoon

45ml vodka

15ml blue curacao

125ml lemonade

maraschino cherry

orange slice

1   Combine liquid ingredients in a collins or highball glass filled with ice cubes. Stir well. Garnish with the cherry and orange slice.

Makes 1

Bullfrog

45ml vodka

15ml triple sec

170ml lemonade or limeade

slice of lemon or lime to garnish

1 Pour the vodka, triple sec and lemonade or limeade into a collins glass filled with ice and stir well. Garnish with a lemon or lime slice.

Makes 1

Cape Cod

30ml vodka

cranberry juice

lime wedge

1 Add the vodka to a highball glass filled with ice, then top-up with cranberry juice. Squeeze lime wedge into glass and drop it in.

Makes 1

Dusty Dog

60ml vodka

15ml crème de cassis

1 teaspoon lemon juice

dash bitters

140ml ginger ale

lemon twist

1   Combine liquid ingredients in a cocktail shaker with cracked ice. Shake well and strain into a chilled highball glass almost filled with clean ice cubes. Garnish with the lemon twist.

Makes 1

Caprice Martini

60ml gin

30ml sweet vermouth

30ml campari

1 Combine all ingredients with cracked ice in a cocktail shaker and shake well. Strain into a chilled 90ml martini glass straight up.

Makes 1

Parisian Martini

45ml gin

15ml dry vermouth

1½ teaspoon crème de cassis

1 Combine all ingredients with cracked ice in a cocktail shaker and shake well. Strain into a chilled 90ml martini glass. Garnish with lemon twist.

Makes 1

Puerto Rico Rickey

60ml gin

30ml lime juice

ice cubes

2 dashes raspberry syrup

soda water

lime wheel

1 Pour gin and lime juice over ice into glass. Add the raspberry syrup and top up with soda water. Garnish with a wheel of lime to serve.

Makes 1

Note: Bourbon, rum or whisky can be substituted for gin.

Beer Buster

45ml vodka

2 dashes Tabasco

340ml beer

1 Stir vodka and tobasco together in a chilled beer mug or pint glass. Pour in beer.

Makes 1

Bloody Mary

45ml vodka

1½ teaspoons lemon juice

2 drops worcestershire

2 drops tabasco

salt and pepper to taste

tomato juice

celery stick to garnish

1 Combine liquid ingredients over ice in a highball or collins glass and stir well. Garnish with celery stick, olive, marinated string bean or vegetable of choice. Serve with swizzle stick and straw.

Makes 1

Fuzzy Navel

30ml vodka

30ml peach-tree schnapps

125ml orange juice

orange slice to garnish

1 Combine liquid ingredients in a collins or highball glass filled with ice cubes. Stir well. Garnish with orange slice.

Makes 1

Flying Dutchman

60ml vodka

15ml green crème de menthe

15ml white crème de menthe

lime wedge to garnish

1 Combine all liquid ingredients in a highball or collins glass filled with ice, stir and serve, garnished with lime wedge.

Makes 1

Greyhound

30ml vodka

grapefriut juice

lemon twist to garnish

1 Combine ingredients in a highball or collins glass filled with ice, stir and serve, garnished with lemon twist.

Makes 1

Karoff

45ml vodka

30ml cranberry juice

140ml club soda

lime wedge

1 Combine all liquid ingredients in a highball or collins glass filled with ice and stir well. Garnish with the lime wedge.

Makes 1

Salty Dog

2 teaspoons salt

lime wedge

60ml vodka

140ml grapefruit juice

1 Place the salt in a saucer. Rub the lime wedge around the rim of a highball, then dip the glass into the salt to coat the rim. Almost fill the glass with ice cubes and pour the vodka and grapefruit juice into the glass. Stir well.

Makes 1

finger food from the barbecue

Using the barbecue to cook finger food provides a quick and easy option for casual entertaining. Prepare food in advance and keep it refrigerated until ready to throw on the barbie. It's a sure way to have food cooked fresh and served hot for everyone to enjoy.

Grilled Prawns with Lime and Avocado Oil Vinaigrette

(see photograph on page 32)

LIME AND AVOCADO OIL VINAIGRETTE

1 clove garlic

2 tablespoons lime juice

½ teaspoon shredded lime rind

1 tablespoon white vinegar

¼ teaspoon sugar

¼ cup avocado oil

¼ teaspoon prepared minced chilli

GRILLED PRAWNS

24 raw prawns, tail on

24 small satay sticks

1 tablespoon chopped fresh coriander

1 Crush and peel garlic. Place in a screw-top jar with lime juice, rind, vinegar, sugar, avocado oil and chilli. Shake well to combine. Set aside for flavours to develop.

2 Thread each prawn onto a satay stick so the stick passes through the prawn twice. Cook prawns on a hot, oiled barbecue hot plate for 2 to 3 minutes, turning during cooking, or until prawns are just cooked. The prawns should be soft and succulent, not hard and dry. Place prawns on a platter. Shake vinaigrette and drizzle over prawns. Garnish with coriander.

Makes 24

Mussel Fritters

(see photograph opposite)

15 mussels in the shell

2 eggs

3 tablespoons cornflour

1 teaspoon baking powder

½ teaspoon salt

freshly ground black pepper

1 tablespoon lemon juice

¼ cup chopped gren onions

2 tablespoons oil

lemon wedges

1 Scrub mussels and debeard. Place in a saucepan over a medium heat and cook for about 5 minutes until shells open. Discard any that do not open. Remove mussels from shells and chop roughly. Beat eggs. Add cornflour, baking powder, salt, pepper, lemon juice, green onions and chopped mussels. Heat oil on a heated barbecue hot plate.

2 Cook tablespoonsful of mixture until golden on both sides. Garnish with lemon wedges and serve.

Makes 13

Barbecued Mussels with Coconut Salsa

About 48 fresh mussels in the shell

COCONUT SALSA

1 spring onion

½ small red pepper

¼ cup coconut milk

¼ cup desiccated coconut

½ teaspoon prepared minced chilli

1 tablespoon finely chopped fresh or
   preserved lemon grass

1 tablespoon chopped fresh coriander

1 Scrub mussels and debeard. Place mussels on the barbecue and cook over hot coals until mussels open. Discard any mussels that do not open. Break off top shell, reserving one to use as a server for the salsa. Arrange mussels on a platter and serve with Coconut Salsa.

COCONUT SALSA

1 Trim green onion and chop finely. Finely chop pepper. Mix spring onion, pepper, coconut milk, coconut, chilli, lemon grass and coriander together. Serve in a bowl with a mussel shell as a scoop.

Makes 48

Stuffed Baby Squid

16 baby squid

olive oil

STUFFING

1 large tomato

1 French shallot

1 clove garlic

1 tablespoon oil

4 spinach leaves

1 teaspoon oregano

200g fetta

1. Thaw squid. Wash and dry. Fill body cavity with stuffing. Secure end with a toothpick. Brush squid with oil and cook on a hot barbecue for 1 minute each side or until just cooked. Overcooking will toughen squid. Serve hot.

STUFFING

1. Cut tomato in half. Remove core and seeds. Chop flesh into very small dice. Peel shallot and chop finely. Crush, peel and finely chop garlic. Heat oil in a frying pan and saute shallot and garlic for 3 minutes or until clear but not coloured. Shred spinach. Add tomato, oregano and spinach. Cover and cook for 2 minutes. Drain off any liquid from spinach. Crumble in fetta and mix well. Use to stuff squid.

Makes 16

Note: Bags of frozen baby squid are available from good supermarkets, large fish shops or Asian provision stores.

Satay Bouches with Red Pepper Relish

6 skinless, boneless chicken thighs

32 small satay sticks

½ cup readymade tandoori paste

RED CAPSICUM RELISH

½ cup readymade red pepper relish

¼ cup unsweetened natural yoghurt

1 tablespoon chopped fresh coriander

1 Cut chicken thighs so they lie flat then cut into 1cm-wide strips. Thread a strip of chicken on to each satay stick. Spread chicken with tandoori paste. Cook chicken on a hot barbecue plate for 5 minutes or until chicken is cooked. Serve hot with Red Capsicum Relish.

RED PEPPER RELISH

1 Mix red pepper relish, yoghurt and coriander together.

Makes 32

Cut-and-Come-Again Barbecued Salmon

600g piece salmon fillet

1 lemon

Crusty bread to serve

HORSERADISH MAYONNAISE

½ cup mayonnaise

¼ cup horseradish cream

2 tablespoons chopped fresh dill

1 teaspoon grated lemon zest

1 tablespoon lemon juice

1 Pin bone the salmon using tweezers to pull bones from salmon flesh. Run your hand over the surface of the salmon to find the bones. Squeeze lemon juice over salmon. Place skin side down on a hot, greased barbecue plate.

2 Cook, covered, on medium heat for 5 minutes or until salmon is almost cooked. Place on a platter and serve with Horseradish Mayonnaise and crusty bread.

HORSERADISH MAYONNAISE

1 Mix mayonnaise, horseradish cream, dill, lemon zest and lemon juice together until combined.

Serves 10

Proscuitto-Wrapped Pork Fillet

(see photograph opposite)

1 pork fillet about 4cm in diameter

¼ cup basil pesto

10 slices proscuitto

3 tablespoons basil pesto

3 tablespoons hot water

1 Cut pork fillet in half lengthwise. Spread pesto over each piece of pork. Wrap proscuitto around pork fillet to completely cover pesto. Place on a barbecue grill and cook over a medium heat, turning regularly.

2 Cook, covered, on indirect heat for 7 to 8 minutes. Remove cover and cook on direct heat for 2 to 3 minutes. Combine basil pesto and hot water. Serve cut into 1cm slices with basil pesto for dipping.

Makes about 44 slices

This is a great way to feed the multitudes. Proscuitto is a fine-quality raw ham which originated in Parma, Italy. If preferred, bacon can be substituted.

Barbecued Lamb Cutlets with Sweet and Sour Plum Sauce (see photograph opposite)

24 lamb cutlets

Good-quality garlic salt

SWEET AND SOUR PLUM SAUCE

½ cup plum jam

3 tablespoons white vinegar

1 tablespoon wholegrain mustard

1 Sprinkle both sides of lamb cutlets with garlic salt. Place on a hot barbecue grill and cook for 2 to 3 minutes each side or until cutlets are cooked but still pink. Cooking time will depend on the thickness of the cutlets. Serve hot with Sweet and Sour Plum Sauce for dipping.

SWEET AND SOUR PLUM SAUCE

1 Mix plum jam, vinegar and mustard together until well combined.

Makes 24

Little French Burgers

(see photograph opposite)

36 x 1cm-thick slices French bread

oil

250g sausage meat

250g lean mince

½ teaspoon salt

freshly ground black pepper

1 cup apple sauce

1 tablespoon wholegrain mustard

small salad greens

1 Brush bread slices with oil. Mix sausage meat, mince, salt and pepper together. Take heaped tablespoonsful and form into patties. Cook patties on a hot barbecue for 3 minutes each side or until golden and cooked. Place bread slices on barbecue and cook each side until lightly golden. Mix apple sauce and mustard together.

TO SERVE

1 Place small salad greens on a piece of toasted French bread. Top with apple sauce, a meat pattie and then another piece of toasted bread. Serve immediately.

Makes 18

New Potato Snacks

24 small new potatoes, about
  2½ to 3cm in diameter

24 x 6cm stalks rosemary

oil spray

salt

AIOLI

2 cloves garlic

1 teaspoon Dijon mustard

¾ cup mayonnaise

1 Scrub potatoes. Cook in boiling water for 5 to 7 minutes or until almost cooked but still firm. Drain and cool. Strip rosemary of leaves to about 4cm from the end. Thread a potato on each rosemary stalk. Spray potatoes with oil and sprinkle lightly with salt. Place on a hot barbecue grill and cook for 5 to 10 minutes or until potatoes are golden and cooked. Serve with Aioli.

AIOLI

1 Crush, peel and very finely chop garlic. Mix garlic and mustard into mayonnaise.

Makes 24

Korean Barbecued Beef

600g rump steak

MARINADE

2 cloves garlic

¼ cup soy sauce

1 tablespoon sesame oil

1 tablespoon prepared minced ginger

2 tablespoons toasted sesame seeds

NECTARINE SALSA

2 nectarines

3 spring onions

1 tablespoon vinegar

2 tablespoons toasted sesame seeds

TO SERVE

35 small pieces lettuce

1 Freeze meat until firm but not frozen. This makes slicing easier. Cut into very thin slices. Marinate for an hour in marinade at room temperature or overnight in the refrigerator. Heat a barbecue hot plate until very hot. Drop meat slices onto hot plate and cook each side quickly for 30 seconds to 1 minute.

MARINADE

1 Crush, peel and finely chop garlic. Mix garlic, soy sauce, sesame oil, ginger and sesame seeds together.

NECTARINE SALSA

1 Destone nectarines and cut flesh into very small dice. Wash and trim spring onions. Cut into quarters lengthwise and chop very finely. Mix nectarine, spring onions, vinegar and sesame seeds together.

TO SERVE

1 Wash and dry lettuce. Serve hot meat on a piece of lettuce topped with Nectarine Salsa.

Makes 35

Grilled Sea Scallop in Cos Spears

450–650g sea scallops (approximately 12 scallops)

¼ cup couscous, cooked and fluffed

3 tablespoons orange juice

2 tablespoon olive oil

3 mixed baby cos leaves

2 blood oranges, peeled and segmented (squeeze and reserve juice)

60g baby green beans, cleaned and cooked

1 large tomato, cored and diced

fresh cracked black pepper to taste

1 Coat scallops in cooked couscous. Season and grill scallops. Set aside and allow to cool. In a mixing bowl, combine orange juice and olive oil. Line up spears of baby lettuce leaves, top with sea scallops, blood orange segments, green beans and tomato.

2 Season with fresh black cracked pepper and drizzle with dressing.

Makes 12 pieces

Baby Octopus Marinated in Olive Oil and Oregano

⅓ cup olive oil

zest of 1 lemon

2 tablespoons lemon juice

⅓ cup French shallots, finely sliced

2 teaspoons oregano, chopped

freshly ground black pepper and salt

750g baby octopus, cleaned

salad leaves, for serving

1 In a bowl, mix together the olive oil, lemon zest, lemon juice, shallots, oregano, and pepper and salt. Add the octopus, and leave to marinate for 1 hour. Heat a chargrill pan, lightly brush with oil, add octopus, and cook, basting with marinade for 2–3 minutes, or until tender. Serve on a bed of salad leaves.

Serves 4

Chermoula Prawns

24 raw prawns, heads and shells removed

¼ small red onion, roughly chopped

2 cloves garlic, roughly chopped

⅓ cup coriander

⅓ cup mint

⅓ cup flat-leaf parsley

1 small red chilli, deseeded and chopped

1 teaspoon ground cumin

½ teaspoon sweet paprika

2 tablespoons lime juice

2 tablespoons olive oil

2 limes, cut into wedges

1 Soak 8 bamboo skewers in water for 30 minutes. Remove veins from prawns. Thread 3 prawns onto each skewer and place in a shallow dish.

2 Place onion, garlic, coriander, mint, parsley, chilli, cumin, paprika, lime juice and olive oil in a food processor. Process until smooth. Coat prawns in marinade, cover with cling wrap and refrigerate for 3–4 hours.

3 Cook prawns on a barbecue grill or char-grill for 2–3 minutes or until cooked. Serve with lime wedges.

Makes 8

Apricot and Sausage Kebabs

5 thin pork sausages

125g dried apricots

¾ cup apricot marinade or honey chilli marinade

20 mini bamboo satay sticks, soaked

1 Par-grill the sausages carefully, turning frequently so they remain straight. Remove and allow to cool.

2 When cold, cut each into 4 even pieces. Thread lengthwise onto the soaked satay skewers alternating with apricot.

3 Prepare barbecue for medium-high direct cooking. Place a sheet of baking paper over grill bars or grill plate. Brush the kebabs with apricot marinade or other and cook turning frequently and brushing with marinade until cooked and well glazed, about 8–10 minutes. Serve immediately.

Makes 20

Apricot Bacon and Banana Bites

3 large firm bananas

4 rashers bacon

¾ cup apricot marinade

wooden cocktail sticks, soaked

1 Cut bananas into 35mm slices at an angle. Cut bacon into 10cm long strips.

2 Wrap a strip of bacon around each banana piece, secure with a cocktail stick. Place on a tray and brush with the marinade.

3 Prepare barbecue for medium direct heat; oil the grill bars or grill plate. When ready, place a sheet of cooking paper on the bars or plate.

4 Arrange the bananas in rows on the baking paper. Cook for 10 minutes, brushing with extra marinade and turning frequently with tongs, until bacon is cooked.

Serves 4

Barbecue Oysters in Chilli Sauce

12 oysters in the half shell

1 tablespoon unsalted butter

½ teaspoon crushed garlic

2 tablespoons lemon juice

2 tablespoons chilli sauce

pared lemon zest to garnish

chilli flakes to garnish

1   In a small pan, melt the butter, add the garlic and cook just until the butter colours. Remove from heat, add the lemon juice and chilli sauce, stir to combine.

2   Prepare a metal tray (eg Swiss roll tin) with a layer of cooking salt about 1cm deep. Transport sauce, tray and oysters to the barbecue.

3   Place the tray of salt on grill over direct high heat. When salt has heated well, remove to the side. Place the oysters in the tin, pushing shells into the salt to prevent them tipping. With a teaspoon spoon sauce over each oyster. Replace the tray on the grill and cook for 5–6 minutes or until sauce around the oyster bubbles. Remove immediately and serve garnished with lemon zest and chilli flakes.

Serves 3–4

Note: For larger quantities of oysters adjust sauce quantity per 6 or 12 oysters.

Barbecued Stuffed Mushrooms

12 medium sized mushrooms about
  4–5cm in diameter

3 rashers bacon, rind removed and
  chopped

2 tablespoons fresh breadcrumbs

3 tablespoons salsa dip

½ teaspoon parsley flakes

feta cheese, crumbed

1 Remove the stems from the mushrooms, trim off end of stem and finely chop the stems.

2 Heat a frying pan, add bacon and cook until the fat runs. Add the mushroom stems and continue to cook the bacon and stems. Stir in the breadcrumbs, salsa and parsley flakes. Remove from heat and set aside.

3 Remove the skin from the mushrooms and brush mushrooms with olive oil. Stuff the mushroom caps with the stuffing. Place on a tray; sprinkle each mushroom with crumbled feta, pressing gently on. Take to barbecue.

4 Place mushrooms onto greased grill bars over direct hot heat with hood down and cook for 8 to 10 minutes. If barbecue has no hood or lid, improvise by inverting a baking dish over the mushrooms so the cheese will cook.

Serves 12

Chicken Satay

12 bamboo skewers

500g chicken thigh fillets, diced (beef, lamb and pork can also be used)

2 tablespoons peanut oil

2 tablespoons sweet soy sauce (kecap manis)

1 tablespoon soy sauce

1 clove garlic, crushed

1 Soak bamboo skewers in cold water for 15–20 minutes.

2 Thread diced chicken onto bamboo skewers. Place chicken in a large dish. Combine peanut oil, kecap manis, soy sauce and garlic. Pour marinade over chicken and leave to marinate in the refrigerator for 1–2 hours.

3 Cook satays on a barbecue for 10–15 minutes or until cooked.

4 Serve with quick peanut sauce.

Makes about 12

Garlic Pepper Prawns

24 large raw prawns

6 cloves crushed garlic

1 teaspoon freshly ground black
peppercorns

½ cup extra virgin olive oil

freshly ground sea salt to taste

1 Peel and devein the prawns and place in a large glass bowl with the remaining ingredients. Cover and marinate for 1 hour in the refridgerator stirring a few times to develop the flavours then cover and refrigerate.

2 Preheat BBQ hotplate and place a sheet of baking paper to cover the surface area.

3 Cook the prawns with some of the marinade for a few minutes each side – be careful not to overcook the prawns.

4 Add a small amount of the marinade during the cooking if required.

Serves 4

Herbed Fish Kebabs

16 small bay leaves

¼ cup extra virgin olive oil

finely grated zest of 1 lemon

¼ cup lemon juice

½ teaspoon garlic salt

1 teaspoon parsley flakes

¼ small bunch chives, chopped

1 tablespoon capers, drained and chopped

freshly ground black pepper

800g thick boneless fish fillets, cut into 3cm pieces

2 red onions, cut into wedges

1 Soak 8 bamboo skewers in water for 30 minutes. Soak the bay leaves in hot water for 10 minutes.

2 Combine the olive oil, lemon zest and juice, garlic salt, parsley, chives, capers and pepper in a bowl.

3 Thread 5 pieces of fish onto each skewer, alternating with a bay leaf and a piece of onion. Place in a large shallow dish. Brush with the marinade to coat. Cover with cling wrap and marinate for 10–15 minutes in the refrigerator.

4 Cook the kebabs on the barbecue or chargrill, basting from time to time, for 5–6 minutes or until cooked. Serve with lemon wedges and a tossed salad.

Serves 4

Note: Bamboo skewers should be soaked in water for 30 minutes – this stops the skewer from burning on the barbecue. The ideal fish for kebabs are blue-eye cod, ling or flake fillets.

Honey and Chilli Prawn Skewers

1kg medium sized raw king prawns

½ cup honey and chilli marinade

mixed salad greens for serving

8 bamboo skewers, soaked

1 Shell the prawns leaving the tails on; devein the prawns. Place in a ceramic dish and pour over the marinade. Toss to coat all prawns, cover and marinate in the refrigerator for 1 hour or more.

2 Thread 3 prawns onto each skewer through 2 sides.

3 Prepare barbecue for medium high direct cooking.

4 Place a sheet of baking paper over the hot grill bars or grill plate and place on the skewered prawns. Cook for 2–3 minutes each side, brushing with marinade as they cook. They will turn pink when cooked.

Makes 8

Lemon Potato Wedges

4–6 medium sized potatoes, peeled

1 teaspoon freshly crushed garlic

3 tablespoons olive oil

½ cup water

½ teaspoon lemon pepper

⅓ cup fresh lemon juice

salt

1   Halve the potatoes then cut each half into 4–6 wedges. Place into a large bowl. Mix garlic, oil, water and lemon juice together, pour over potatoes and toss well to coat. Place in a shallow baking dish in a single layer, sprinkle with lemon pepper.

2   Cook over direct heat in a covered barbecue. Cook for 20 minutes, turn after 10 minutes. Add water if drying out, continue to cook and turn until tender and crisp. Can be moved to indirect heat while other dishes finish cooking.

3   To serve, sprinkle lightly with salt.

Serves 4–6

Peanut Crusted Chicken Satays

(see photograph opposite)

3 chicken breast fillets, about 300g each

1½ cups satay marinade

¾ cup crushed unsalted roasted peanuts

20 bamboo skewers, soaked

1 continental cucumber pared into ribbons with a vegetable peeler to garnish

1   Remove the breast bone if present. Place fillets, smooth side down between 2 pieces of plastic wrap. Pound with a rolling pin or the side of a meat mallet to flatten slightly and even out the thickness. Cut into 25mm wide strips. Place into a flat non-metallic container. Pour in about ½ cup of marinade, turn to coat both sides and marinate for 2 hours or more in the refrigerator.

2   Weave 1 long strip or 2 short strips onto each skewer, but do not bunch up. Brush both sides with marinade from the container, discard the remainder. Refrigerate until ready to cook. Take 1 cup fresh marinade, place in a bowl to use for brushing during cooking. Take to the barbecue.

3   Prepare the barbecue for direct heat cooking. Place the skewers on well-oiled grill bars or grill plate. Cook for 2 minutes on each side, brushing often with the marinade.

4   Place a piece of foil on a flat tray and sprinkle over the crushed peanuts. As satays come off the grill, press each side onto the peanuts and place on a warmed platter. Garnish with cucumber ribbons. If desired, mix ¾ cup fresh marinade with 2 tablespoons lemon or lime juice and use as extra sauce.

Makes about 18

Teriyaki Calamari Skewers

(not photographed)

2 large calamari tubes, cleaned, cut into 5mm-thick rings

TERIYAKI SAUCE

1 French shallot, thinly sliced

1cm piece fresh ginger, minced

¼ cup rice wine vinegar or sherry

2 tablespoons reduced-salt soy sauce

1 teaspoon honey

2 tablespoons lime or lemon juice

1 teaspoon sesame oil

1   Soak 24 small or 8 large bamboo skewers in cold water for at least 20 minutes.

2   Preheat a barbecue or grill to a high heat.

3   Cut each calamari ring in half. Thread strips onto bamboo skewers in an 'S' shape – use 1 strip on small skewers and 3 strips on large skewers.

4   Place skewers on barbecue or under grill. Cook, turning several times, for 1–2 minutes or until calamari is just cooked.

TERIYAKI SAUCE

1   Place shallot, ginger, vinegar, soy sauce, honey and 1 tablespoon of lime juice in a small saucepan over medium heat. Stir in sesame oil and remaining lime juice. Serve with skewers.

Makes 24

short and stunning

Shaken, sipped through a straw or just stirred, there's a certain easy sophistication about a mixed drink served in a beautiful glass. Whatever your preference, drinks are simple to prepare with a range of flavours and alcohol bases to choose from, depending on what you have on hand. Don't be afraid to substitute and experiment with different flavours.

Passionfruit Pointers

(see photograph on page 58)

2 x 230g jars passionfruit in syrup
500ml vodka

1 Mix passionfruit syrup and vodka together. Pour into a clean, dry bottle and seal with a cork or stopper. Place in the freezer until ready to serve. Serve in chilled shot glasses.

Makes 10–15

Peach Breeze

(top left)

2 parts gin
1 part peach schnapps
ice
cranberry juice
red grapefruit juice
lime twist to garnish

1 Pour gin and peach schnapps into a glass over ice. Fill the remainder of the glass with cranberry and grapefruit juice. Garnish with a lime twist.

Makes 1

Martini

(bottom left)

45ml gin or vodka
5ml dry vermouth
lemon twist
olive

1 Pour gin or vodka and dry vermouth into a mixing bowl or jug. Add ice. Stir and strain into a chilled glass. Run a lemon twist around the rim of the glass. Garnish with a lemon twist and an olive if wished.

Makes 1

Black Russian

(top right)

30ml vodka
30ml kahlua
cola
cherry

1 Pour vodka over crushed ice then add kahlua. Top with cola if wished. Garnish with a cherry.

Makes 1

Side Car

(bottom right)

30ml brandy
30ml cointreau
30ml lemon juice
ice
lemon twist

1 Pour brandy, cointreau, lemon juice and some ice into a shaker. Shake and strain into a glass. Garnish with a lemon twist.

Makes 1

Red Eye

(left)

30ml rum

125ml raspberry cordial

ice

orange slice to garnish

cherry to garnish

1 Pour rum and raspberry cordial over ice in a glass. Garnish with an orange slice and a cherry.

Makes 1

Illusion

(right)

15ml vodka

15ml triple sec o cointreau

30ml melon liqueur

45ml lemon juice

15ml lime juice

lime or lemon wedge

1 Pour vodka, Triple Sec, melon liqueur, and lemon and lime juice into a shaker. Shake and strain into a glass. Garnish with a wedge of lime or melon.

Makes 1

Kamikaze

30ml vodka

30ml triple sec or cointreau

30ml fresh lemon juice

1 teaspoon lime cordial

orange slice

1 Pour vodka, triple sec, lemon juice and lime cordial into a shaker. Shake and strain into a glass. Garnish with an orange slice.

Makes 1

Cosmopolitan

45ml vodka

15ml triple sec or cointreau

15ml lemon juice

30ml cranberry juice

orange peel

1 Pour vodka, triple sec, lemon juice and cranberry juice into a shaker. Shake and strain into a glass. Garnish with a twist of orange peel.

Makes 1

Bewitched

15ml vodka

15ml benedictine and brandy

15ml cream

1 Combine ingredients in a mixing glass with ice. Stir gently and strain into a large shot glass or cordial glass.

Makes 1

Campari Vodkatini

45ml vodka

1½ teaspoons campari

lime twist

1 Combine liquid ingredients with cracked ice in a cocktail shaker and shake well. Strain into a chilled cocktail glass and garnish with lime twist.

Makes 1

Fools Gold

15ml vodka

15ml galliano

1 Combine the ingredients in a shaker filled with ice, shake and strain into a shot glass.

Makes 1

Apple Margaritas

lemon slice

salt

30ml calvados

30ml grand marnier rouge

30ml grenadine

30ml lemon juice

30ml tequila

ice

lemon slices, extra, to garnish

1   Rub margarita glass rims with lemon slice and frost with salt. Combine liquid ingredients with ice; shake well. Strain drink into prepared glasses. Garnish each glass with a lemon slice and serve.

Makes 3

Banana Margarita

lemon or lime slice

salt

45ml tequila

30ml lime or lemon juice

30ml banana liqueur

15ml triple sec or cointreau

ice

banana slice, to garnish

1 Rub margarita glass rim with lime or lemon slice and frost with salt. Combine liquid ingredients with ice; shake well. Strain drink into glass. Garnish with banana slice and serve.

Makes 1

Chocolate Raspberry Martini

45ml vodka

15ml chocolate liqueur

splash of soda

raspberry to garnish

1 Combine vodka and chocolate liquer ingredients in a cocktail shaker with cracked ice. Shake well and strain into a chilled 90ml martini glass. Top with a splash of soda. Garnish with a fresh raspberry.

Makes 1

Deliberation

45ml vodka

15ml melon liqueur

lemon and lime twist to garnish

1 Combine ingredients in a mixing glass filled with ice cubes. Stir well and strain into a 90ml martini glass and garnish lemon and lime twist.

Makes 1

Frozen Mango Margarita

45ml silver tequila

30ml triple sec or cointreau

45ml lemon juice, freshly squeezed

60ml simple syrup or sweet-and-sour
  mix (see below)

¾ cup partially frozen mango,
  unsweetened (preferably individual
  quick frozen or fresh)

ice

mango slice, to garnish

SUGAR SYRUP

60 ml water

1 cup sugar

SWEET AND SOUR MIX

3 cups water

3 cups granulated sugar

2 cups fresh lemon juice

2 cups fresh lime juice

1 Prepare glasses by rubbing margarita glass rim with lime wedge and frost
   with sugar. Mix all liquid ingredients with mango and cracked ice in a
   blender and blend until slushy. Pour cocktail into a chilled prepared margarita
   glass. Garnish with mango slice.

Makes 1

Frozen Strawberry Margaritas

lime or lemon slices

salt

¾ cup tequila

60ml triple sec or cointreau

¼ cup frozen limeade concentrate

1 cup frozen strawberries

8 cups crushed ice

lime or lemon slices, extra, to garnish

1 Rub margarita glass rim with lime or lemon slice and frost with salt. Combine ingredients in a blender and process until slushy. Pour drink into prepared glasses. Garnish with lime or lemon slice and serve.

Makes 4

Gates of Hell

45ml tequila

2 teaspoon lemon juice, freshly squeezed

2 teaspoon lime juice, freshly squeezed

crushed ice

1 teaspoon cherry brandy, for drizzling

1 Combine all ingredients, except cherry brandy, in a shaker. Shake well. Strain into an old-fashioned glass almost filled with crushed ice. Drizzle the cherry brandy over the top.

Makes 1

Jumping Margarita

slice of lime plus 1 to garnis

salt

45ml tequila

30ml triple sec

45ml margarita mix

15ml lime juice

90ml lemonade

ice

1 Rub margarita glass rim with lime slice and frost with salt. Mix the first 5 ingredients in shaker filled with ice; shake well. Strain cocktail into glass. Garnish with lime slice and serve.

Makes 1

Scottie Was Beamed Up

crushed ice

30ml tequila

15ml galiano

lemon twist, to garnish

1   Build over ice into an old-fashioned glass and garnish with a lemon twist.

Makes 1

Cowboy Margarita

1½ cups frozen limeade concentrate

1½ cups tequila

1½ cups beer

ice

1   Place undiluted frozen limeade concentrate in a jug. Fill empty limeade can with tequila and pour into the jug. Fill empty limeade can with beer and pour into the jug. Serve over plenty of ice. Makes about 4 big servings.

Makes 1

Desert Shield

45ml vodka

15ml cranberry liqueur

125ml cranberry juice

1 Combine ingredients in a Collins or highball glass filled with ice cubes. Stir well.

Makes 1

to serve with drinks

Coming up with new ideas for simple, tasty finger food is always a challenge, especially when you don't have the time or don't want to spend all day in the kitchen. The recipes that follow will deliver great taste, are easy to prepare and, if our eating experiences when I wrote this book are anything to go by, total enjoyment!

Mushroom Croustades

(see photograph on page 78)

6 small, rectangular, partly cooked
bread rolls

3 tablespoons olive oil

200g brown mushrooms

1 small onion

1 clove garlic

1 tablespoon olive oil

2 teaspoons shredded lemon zest

1 tablespoon chopped parsley

1 teaspoon fresh thyme leaves or

½ teaspoon dried thyme

3 tablespoons lemon juice

½ teaspoon salt

1 Cut rolls in half lengthwise. Scoop out centre of rolls using a sharp knife. Brush rolls with first measure of oil, inside and out. Bake at 200°C for 5 to 7 minutes or until golden and crisp. Wipe mushrooms and trim stalks if necessary. Cut into thick slices. Peel onion and chop finely. Crush, peel and chop garlic. Heat second measure of oil in a frying pan and saute onion and garlic for 5 minutes or until clear. Add mushrooms and saute for 2 to 3 minutes. Add lemon zest, parsley, thyme, lemon juice and salt.

2 Cook for 2 minutes. Pile mushroom mixture into roll cases. Serve warm.

Makes 12

Note: These are able to be eaten with the fingers and provide something a little more substantial than a mouthful. The rolls used are the ones where you finish the baking at home.

Chorizo Rolls

(see photograph opposite)

4 chorizo sausages

5 sheets filo pastry

¼ cup basil pesto

tomato sauce or tomato relish

1 Remove skin from chorizo and trim ends to flatten. Place filo on a board. Brush each sheet with basil pesto, layering as you go. Place chorizo end to end down the long side of the layered pastry. Roll pastry around chorizo. Place seam side down on a lightly oiled baking tray.

2 Bake at 200°C for 10 minutes or until pastry is lightly golden. Remove from oven and cut into 2cm pieces. Serve warm with tomato sauce or relish.

Makes 15

Note: We used loose chorizo sausages from the supermarket deli cabinet for these rolls. They vary slightly in length but you need about 30cm of sausage for this recipe.

Quick Blini with Smoked Salmon and Horseradish Cream

1 cup plain flour

½ cup wholemeal flour

2 teaspoons baking powder

1 teaspoon sugar

1 egg

1¼ cups milk

2 tablespoons horseradish cream

TOPPING

200g packet smoked salmon

¼ cup horseradish cream

fish roe

chopped parsley

1 Mix flour, wholemeal flour, baking powder and sugar together in a bowl to combine. Lightly beat egg and mix with milk and horseradish cream. Whisk milk mixture into dry ingredients using a fork to form a smooth batter. Lightly oil a frying pan and cook about a level tablespoonsful of mixture until bubbles form. Turn and cook other side before bubbles break. Cook until lightly golden.

2 Warm blini wrapped in foil in the oven or wrapped in a paper towel in the microwave. Top with a piece of smoked salmon, a dollop of horseradish cream and garnish with fish roe and chopped parsley.

Makes 40

Chinese Fish-Stuffed Peppers

6 small green peppers

400g skinned and boned white-fleshed fish fillets

2 green onions

1 teaspoon prepared minced chilli

4 sprigs fresh coriander

2 egg whites

sweet chilli or soy sauce

1 Cut peppers in half, remove seeds and core. Cut each half into four. Blanch in boiling water for 2 minutes. Drain and run under cold water. Drain well. Cut fish into smaller pieces. Cut spring onions into thirds.

2 Place fish, green onions, chilli, coriander and egg whites in the bowl of a food processor. Process until mixture is paste-like. Fill capsicum quarters with fish mixture. Arrange in an ovenproof dish. Cover with foil and bake at 180°C for 15 minutes or until fish is set. Serve warm with sweet chilli or soy sauce for dipping.

Makes 32

Proscuitto-Wrapped Melon

(see photograph opposite)

½ honeydew melon

½ rockmelon

9 slices proscuitto

1 Remove seeds and peel melons. Cut melons into thin lengthwise wedges. Cut each wedge in half again crosswise. Cut proscuitto into pieces large enough to wrap around fruit wedges.

2 Wrap around fruit and arrange in alternate colours on a serving platter. Chill until ready to serve.

Makes 26 pieces

Grilled Tuscan Pepper Rolls

(see photograph opposite)

3 mixed red and yellow peppers

90g jar anchovy fillets

½ cup drained capers

¼ cup olive oil

1 sprig fresh rosemary

1 clove garlic

1 Cut peppers in half, remove core and seeds and place cut side down on an oven tray. Grill until skins are black. Remove from oven and peel when cool enough to handle. Drain anchovies and chop roughly with capers, mixing together to combine. Cut peppers into lengthwise strips about 1 ½ to 2cm wide. Place about ½ teaspoon of anchovy mixture at one end of the pepper strip and roll up, securing with a toothpick.

2 Place in a bowl and pour olive oil over. Wash rosemary and add to bowl. Crush, peel and chop garlic and add to bowl. Refrigerate for up to 3 days until ready to serve. Serve with crusty Italian bread.

Makes 35

Note: Make these in advance and use on an antipasto platter.

Marinated Mushrooms

(see photograph opposite)

200g brown button mushrooms

2 cloves garlic

¼ cup olive oil

1 tablespoon shredded lemon zest

1 tablespoon fresh thyme leaves

2 tablespoons balsamic vinegar

freshly ground black pepper

1 Wipe mushrooms with a damp cloth and trim stalks if necessary. Crush, peel and finely chop garlic. Place garlic, mushrooms, oil, lemon zest, thyme and vinegar in a bowl. Mix gently to combine. Grind black pepper over. Cover and refrigerate for 1 to 2 days to marinate before serving.

Serves 6–8

Note: If mushrooms are more than bite-sized, cut into quarters.

Japanese-Style Fish with Wasabi Mayonnaise

3 skinned and boned white-fleshed fish fillets

2 egg whites

1 teaspoon baking powder

½ cup cornflour

2 tablespoons mirin (Japanese sweet rice wine)

1 tablespoon black sesame seeds

oil for frying

WASABI MAYONNAISE

½ teaspoon wasabi powder

1 tablespoon mirin

½ cup lite mayonnaise

¼ teaspoon sesame oil

1   Cut fish into pieces 4cm to 5cm long. Beat egg whites with a fork until broken up and lightly foamed. Mix in baking powder, cornflour, mirin and sesame seeds until combined. Heat about 2cm of oil in a frying pan. Dip fish pieces in egg white mixture, draining off excess. Cook in hot oil, turning to cook both sides, for about 4 minutes or until fish is cooked and batter golden. Serve hot with Wasabi Mayonnaise.

2   Mix wasabi powder and mirin together until smooth. Mix with mayonnaise and sesame oil.

Serves 4

Linda's Favourite Curry Turnovers

4 sheets unsweetened short pastry

400g can potatoes

¼ cup onion marmalade

3 tablespoons chopped fresh coriander

1 teaspoon red curry paste

paprika

1 Roll pastry a little thinner. Cut five 9cm-diameter circles from each pastry sheet. Cut circles in half. Drain potatoes and cut into small pieces. Mix with onion marmalade, coriander and curry paste. Place a teaspoon of potato mixture on each semicircle. Wet pastry edges and fold dough over to form a cone shape.

2 Place on an oven tray. Cover with a damp tea towel while preparing remaining turnovers. Bake at 200°C for 15 minutes, turning after 10 minutes. Dust with paprika before serving.

Makes 40

Note: If readymade onion marmalade or relish is unavailable, use your favourite relish or chutney instead.

Casalie Chicken Liver Crostini

(see photograph opposite)

36 x 1cm-wide slices Italian bread

3 cloves garlic

1 small onion

300g chicken livers

2 tablespoons olive oil

3 tablespoons marsala

1 tablespoon chopped fresh sage or
   1½ teaspoons dried sage

3 tablespoons drained capers

salt

freshly ground black pepper

fresh sage and chopped parsley to
   garnish

1 Grill or bake bread slices until golden on both sides. Crush and peel garlic and use one clove to rub over crostini. Chop remaining garlic finely. Peel and finely chop onion. Wash and dry chicken livers. Heat oil in a frying pan and saute onion and garlic for 5 minutes or until clear. Add chicken livers and stir fry for 2 minutes. Add marsala and sage and cook for a further 3 to 4 minutes or until livers are just soft but still slightly pink. Add capers and remove from heat. Process in a food processor until finely chopped.

2 Season with salt and pepper. Refrigerate until required. When ready to serve, heat liver mixture quickly in a frying pan and pile on top of crostini. Garnish with fresh sage and chopped parsley.

Makes 36

Note: I always think a platter of crostini is hard to beat as food to serve with drinks. We sometimes serve these as an entree with tomato and basil-topped crostini. I'm not that fussed on liver but, eaten like this, it's a total taste treat.

Pizza Toasts

(see photograph opposite)

1 French baguette

¼ cup olive tapenade

20 slices salami

120g mozzarella cheese

3 medium tomatoes

freshly ground black pepper

olive oil

8 large basil leaves

1 Cut baguette in half lengthwise. Grill both sides of bread until lightly golden. Spread cut sides with tapenade and place on an oven tray. Remove skin from salami and arrange slices on top of tapenade. Slice mozzarella thinly and place on salami. Slice tomatoes and place on cheese. Grind pepper over, drizzle with olive oil and grill for 2 to 3 minutes or until cheese has melted. Garnish with torn basil leaves and cut into 3cm slices on the diagonal.

Makes about 40 slices

Note: Some of the simplest things are the ones that are most enjoyed. Try these when you require something a little more filling.

Pumpkin and Roasted Pepper Dip or Spread

200g piece seeded pumpkin

1 roasted red pepper

1 teaspoon prepared minced chilli

2 tablespoons olive oil

½ teaspoon salt

freshly ground black pepper

1 Wrap unpeeled pumpkin in a piece of plastic wrap and microwave on high power for 5 to 8 minutes or until cooked. Carefully remove from wrap. Remove skin and place flesh in a blender or food processor.

2 Roughly chop red pepper and add to blender or processor with chilli and olive oil. Blend or process until smooth. Season to taste with salt and pepper. Serve with pita crisps or bread slices.

Makes 1½ cups

Thai Spiced Nuts

3 cups mixed nuts, such as peanuts, cashews and pecans

2 tablespoons peanut oil

1 tablespoon Thai red curry paste

1 teaspoon hot curry powder

1 Place nuts in a roasting dish. Mix oil, curry paste and curry powder together and toss through nuts. Roast at 180°C for 10 minutes or until lightly golden. Remove from oven and cool. When cold, store in an airtight container.

Makes 3 cups

punches

A well-mixed punch provides an easy drink solution for many occasions. With or without alcohol, chilled or warm, a well garnished punch served in a bowl or jug makes serving drinks to a group of people a delicious and easy option.

Cosmo Punch

(see photograph on page 92)

1 cup tequila

½ cup triple sec or cointreau

½ cup lime cordial

5 cups cranberry juice

lime slices to garnish

ice to garnish

1 Mix tequila, triple sec, lime cordial and cranberry juice together in a bowl or large jug. Garnish with lime slices and ice. Serve chilled.

Makes 7 cups

Non-Alcoholic Tropical Fruit Punch

(see photograph opposite)

500ml orange and mango juice

500ml pineapple juice

165g can coconut milk

1 litre bottle sparkling lime-flavoured mineral water

ice cubes

sprigs fresh mint to garnish

fresh pineapple to garnish

1 Pour juices, coconut milk and mineral water into a bowl or large jug. Add ice cubes and whisk with a metal whisk to combine. Garnish with sprigs of mint and fresh pineapple. Serve chilled.

Makes about 12 litres

Classic Kiwi Punch

(see photograph opposite)

5 kiwifruit

100ml melon liqueur

100ml triple sec or cointreau

250ml gin

1.5 litres lemonade

melon balls to garnish

ice to garnish

1 Peel and puree kiwifruit. Pour kiwifruit, melon liqueur, triple sec, gin and lemonade into a bowl or jug. Garnish with melon balls and ice. Serve chilled.

Makes about 12 litres

Fruit Tea Punch

4 lemon tea bags

4 cups boiling water

1 cinnamon stick

1 tablespoon whole allspice

1 cup sugar

1 cup pineapple juice

750ml bottle white wine

10 ice cubes

6 lemon and orange slices

4 sprigs fresh mint

1   Place tea bags, boiling water, cinnamon stick, allspice and sugar in a large saucepan. Bring to the boil, them remove from the heat. Cool. Strain into a jug and add pineapple juice and white wine. Add ice cubes, lemon and orange slices and sprigs of mint. Stir before pouring. Serve chilled. ⸝

Makes about 2 litres

Mimosa Punch

2 litres orange juice

250ml triple sec or cointreau

2 bottles asti riccadonna

orange slices to garnish

ice to garnish

1   Pour orange juice, triple sec and asti riccadonna into a bowl or large jug. Mix to combine. Garnish with orange slices and ice. Serve chilled.

Makes about 4 litres

Pinkies Punch

250ml gin

125ml triple sec or cointreau

750ml pink grapefruit juice

750ml sparkling lemon

lime slices to garnish

ice to garnish

1   Pour gin, triple sec, grapefruit juice and sparkling lemon into a bowl or large jug. Garnish with lime slices and ice. Serve chilled.

Makes about 2 litres

Cranberry Christmas Punch

2 cups vodka

4 cups cranberry juice

1½ cups rose's lime cordial

2 cups water

3 tablespoons sugar

1   Combine all ingredients in a large punch bowl. Add a large block of ice to keep it all cool.

Serves 20

Red Wine Punch (Sangria)

8 whole cloves

2 cinnamon sticks

2 tablespoons caster sugar

750ml bottle red wine

1 orange, sliced

1 lemon, sliced

500ml soda water

500ml lemonade

1 Combine the whole cloves, cinnamon stick, sugar and 1 cup of the red wine in a saucepan. Stir over low heat until the sugar dissolves. Simmer for 3–4 minutes to extract the flavours from the spices. Pour into a jug with the remaining red wine, orange and lemon slices. Place in the fridge to chill.

2 Before serving strain the red wine and discard cloves and cinnamon quill before adding the chilled soda water and lemonade.

3 Serve with ice cubes.

Makes 1.75 litres

Note: If you prefer the sangria sweeter, add more sugar. You can also add orange juice and pineapple juice. The longer you leave the spices and fruit the more flavour. Add the soda water and lemonade just before serving.

tea and coffee with attitude

Spike a simple cup of tea or well-flavoured coffee with a little alcohol, serve it with a sweet morsel and who needs dessert? Here are some simple, great-tasting ideas for a dessert option with no-fuss preparation and assured success.

Baileys Orange Coffee

(see photograph on page 100)

30ml whisky and cream liqueur

15ml orange-flavoured liqueur

1 cup coffee

frothy milk or whipped cream

pinch nutmeg

1 Pour cream liqueur and orange-flavoured liqueur into a coffee cup or mug. Top with hot coffee and frothy milk or cream if wished. Sprinkle with nutmeg.

Makes 1

Orange and Pistachio Biscotti

(see photograph on page 100)

2½ cups plain flour

1 teaspoon baking powder

1 cup sugar

4 eggs

1 tablespoon grated orange zest

1 cup shelled, roughly chopped pistachio nuts

1 Sift flour and baking powder into a bowl. Mix in sugar. Lightly beat eggs and orange zest together. Pour into a well in the centre of the dry ingredients. Add pistachio nuts and mix until combined. Form dough into three 3cm-diameter logs. Place on a greased and floured oven tray. Bake at 200°C for 15 minutes. Cool. Cut logs into 1cm-wide slices. Place slices on an oven tray and bake at 180°C for a further 15 to 20 minutes to dry biscotti out. Store in an airtight container and serve with Baileys Orange Coffee.

Makes about 80 pieces

Coffee and Walnut Surprises

(see photograph opposite)

250g butter

½ cup sugar

2 tablespoons baileys irish cream

1 cup chopped walnuts

2 tablespoons instant coffee powder

2 cups flour

icing sugar

1 Melt butter in a saucepan large enough to mix all the ingredients. Remove from the heat and stir in sugar, Irish cream liqueur and walnuts. Sift in coffee and flour and mix to combine. Chill until firm enough to handle. Measure tablespoonsful of mixture and roll into balls. Place on a baking-paper-covered baking tray. Bake at 190°C for 12 to 15 minutes or until firm. Cool for 5 minutes then toss lightly in icing sugar. Serve with tea or coffee and a glass of Irish cream liqueur.

Serves 4

Hot Toboggan

(see photograph opposite)

30ml dark rum

15ml butterscotch schnapps

1 teaspoon sugar

1 slice lemon

1 cup hot tea

piece of cinnamon stick

1 Pour rum and butterscotch schnapps into a cup or mug. Add sugar and lemon then pour hot tea over. Mix with a piece of cinnamon stick.

Makes 1

Special Coffee

1 cup strong hot coffee

2 tablespoons brandy

50ml whipped cream

1 cinnamon stick

ground cinnamon

1 Fill a tall coffee cup with coffee. Stir in brandy. Take two tablespoons and use one to gently slide whipped cream off the other and into the cup. Top with a cinnamon stick and a sprinkle of cinnamon. Add sugar if wished. Serve immediately.

Makes 1

Hot Chocolate Toddy

30ml brandy

1 cup hot chocolate

whipped cream

ground nutmeg

chocolate curls

1 Add brandy to mug. Fill with hot chocolate and then top with whipped cream, nutmeg and chocolate curls. Serve immediately.

Makes 1

Green Tea Cooler

1 cup hot green tea

30ml vodka

2 heaped tablespoons lemon and lime
  frozen yoghurt or vanilla ice cream

orange slice to garnish

1 Mix green tea and vodka together. Place 1 heaped tablespoon of frozen
yoghurt in a glass. Pour green tea mixture over. Top with remaining frozen
yoghurt and garnish with orange slice.

Makes 1

Mexican Hot Chocolate

(see photograph opposite)

1 cup hot chocolate

30ml tequila

30ml whisky and liqueur cream

pinch ground nutmeg or chocolate curls
  to garnish

1   Prepare your favourite hot chocolate mix. Pour tequila and Irish cream liqueur into a cup or mug. Pour hot chocolate over. Garnish with nutmeg or chocolate curls.

Makes 1

Note: Make the hot chocolate frothy by either using an espresso machine or frothing the hot milk in a coffee plunger. Alternatively, top with whipped cream.

Linzer Lovelies

(see photograph opposite)

125g butter

½ cup sugar

1 tablespoon golden syrup

1 teaspoon vanilla essence

1¼ cups flour

1 teaspoon baking powder

1 teaspoon cinnamon

½ teaspoon mixed spice

½ cup raspberry jam

1   Melt butter in a saucepan large enough to mix all the ingredients. Mix in sugar and golden syrup. Remove from heat and add vanilla. Sift flour, baking powder, cinnamon and mixed spice into saucepan and mix to combine. Measure teaspoonsful and place on a baking-paper-covered oven tray. Flatten with a fork.

2   Bake at 180°C for 15 minutes or until lightly golden and cooked. Cool on a cooling rack. When cold join two biscuits together with raspberry jam.

Makes 28

Note: For a rich and decadent hot chocolate, melt dark block chocolate in hot milk. Froth extra milk to top the hot chocolate with and garnish with chocolate shavings. Change the Linzer Lovelies to Chocolate Lovelies if preferred. Replace the spices with one tablespoon of cocoa. Fill with chocolate hazelnut spread.

Coffee Moccha

(see photograph opposite)

60g good quality dark chocolate, chopped

½ cup cream

1 cup milk

1½ cups strong black coffee

1 vanilla bean, split in half

¼ teaspoon nutmeg, ground

sugar, to taste

1 Place the chocolate and cream in a saucepan. Stir over low heat until the chocolate melts.

2 Stir in the milk, coffee and vanilla bean. Continue to cook until hot but not boiling.

3 Pour into glasses and serve with a sprinkle of ground nutmeg. Add sugar to taste.

Serves 6

Note: You can vary this recipe to make iced coffee or mocha – just cool down the liquid, add crushed ice, a scoop of ice-cream and enough liquid to blend together. As a winter warmer add a little brandy to the coffee.

Irish Coffee

(not photographed)

GLASS

230ml Irish coffee glass

INGREDIENTS

slice of orange

sugar

45ml Irish whiskey

hot coffee

whipped cream

1 Rub rim of glass with orange and frost with sugar. Pour Irish whiskey into glass and fill to within 15mm of top with the hot coffee. Cover surface to brim with whipped cream.

Serves 1

Amaretto Tea

(not photographed)

GLASS

230ml Irish coffee glass

INGREDIENTS

120ml hot tea

60ml amaretto

1 tablespoon whipped cream

1 Pour hot tea into mug and add amaretto, do not stir. Top with whipped cream.

Serves 1

index